OUT OF HIDING

OUT OF HIDING

poems by
James Lloyd Rice

iUniverse, Inc.
New York Lincoln Shanghai

OUT OF HIDING

iUniverse books may be ordered through booksellers or by contacting:

iUniverse
2021 Pine Lake Road, Suite 100
Lincoln, NE 68512
www.iuniverse.com
1-800-Authors (1-800-288-4677)

ISBN-13: 978-0-595-35873-1 (pbk)
ISBN-13: 978-0-595-80330-9 (ebk)
ISBN-10: 0-595-35873-X (pbk)
ISBN-10: 0-595-80330-X (ebk)

Printed in the United States of America

DEDICATED TO THE MEMORIES OF

Jennifer Lynn Rice   Daughter   1964–1972

Wendy Rice Dreitcer   Niece   1956–2004

Memories of all loved ones who've passed from this life are included in my vivid recall of these bundles of joy, love and grief so intimately shared

AND TO MY LIVING CHILDREN AND THEIR FUTURE PROGENY

Hilary Llewellyn Rice   1982–

Ariana Marie Rice   1986–

CONTENTS

INTRODUCTION

I never imagined a penchant for writing poetry nor dreamed of claiming identity as a poet. I first wrote so I could recall an idea or thought the morning after an evening of excesses. Initially I just scribbled down the idea's content and finding that it often did not recall the fullness of the initial experience. In the cold light of morning such seamy scrawls often failed to reveal the profound series of logical associations from the night before, instead transforming them into silly, incomprehensible gibberish. Then I discovered a poetic style more successful in my attempts to record presumed profundity.

Poems could occasionally weave complex associations into a comprehensible form capable of containing a moment's meaning. The more I wrote, the more frequently this occurred. I believe it was not just a one-way street as I became more skilled in recording my ideas. I think writing poems improves my comprehension and appreciation of the moment. This is why I still write. In writing a poem, my purpose is to grow this moment to its fullest potential.

Writing a poem can enrich the moment of the writing. The poem provides in the moment, a form to faithfully record this same moment. My poems to me are processes of discovery recorded. They reveal to me lost realms of self, clearing them from accumulated debris that had blocked my access, forbidding my experience of rich inner kingdoms. Until hidden territories reveal themselves I am unable to explore and inhabit them. It is as though they don't exist.

My poems often define for me, my personal debris. My addictions, my unseen habit patterns often reveal themselves in my writing. Through my writing I can explore previously secret means and methods whereby my addictions have been able to rob me of rightful space and energy. I become able to explore the rich, full life fully present. An authentic heaven awaits the arrival of consciousness unfettered by secret, old habits. Addictions so discovered provide an opportunity to free myself; a choice to see what has been unseen; hence able to decide how much of the whole I can contain.

INTRODUCTION

continued

I discovered that sometimes others enjoyed my poems so I began to read them to friends and family. Sometimes I was blessed to be asked to read. Other times I willfully inflicted poems upon them and asked for feedback. A few years ago, a good friend put copies of my poems in a binder in her waiting room. People began to ask if I had ever thought of organizing some of my poems into a book. It always seemed an impossible task. How do I select from the hundreds of poems written in thirty years of self-discovery? How do I select poems most likely to please others? Oops! An apparently known addiction, repeatedly discovered, can still block the road. That ancient habit of focusing attention upon pleasing the needs and wishes of others can sometimes obscure my own purpose, intent and interest.

Addiction discovered again and again loses its power to hide possibilities. What seemed impossible becomes possible. I become able to select some of my poems to include in a book. Beyond that, I am sometimes able to experience kingdoms of incalculable wealth abiding right here within me. Infinite possibilities, heretofore unknown, are revealed. Maybe some of my poems can assist others in similar discoveries. Perhaps the muse that flows through me can encourage, support, and even inspire others intentions to encounter covert kingdoms existing within themselves. This is my sincere intention and fond hope.

ACKNOWLEDGEMENTS

I soon discovered that to create a book a writer needs an editor. At the right moment Lynne Blackman, a woman with appropriate skills, significant savvy and surprising interest in the job appeared. Sharing my intention with her has stimulated my paramount efforts to bring my biggest and best self to this project. Lynne, you have my deep respect and gratitude. I needed your attention and appreciation in order to truly believe in this project; for its purpose to become clear; to render credible to this old skeptic its potential to bless others. Thank you for seeing.

Another dear friend who has seen me well is the remarkable artist who sketched my portrait on this book's cover. Even though it was his gift for my sixtieth birthday almost eight years ago (I now have even less hair and no glasses after Lasix procedures) I have never, even in a mirror, seen an image so like me. I am grateful for the countless hours that Jerry Hirshberg worked on this piece. I am grateful too for his generous permission to gild my book with his talented work.

Others see me regularly and well. Their seeing is requisite to my writing. Friends by the dozens in communities of colleagues, ranch partners, Zen sangha brothers and sisters, and other networks too complex to briefly describe, have supported my efforts. They have listened attentively, read works in progress, commented, critiqued and clarified. My joy in reading my poems to others is second only to my joy in writing them.

Weddings, memorial services, anniversaries, birthdays and other special occasions have stirred poetic impulses within me. Family groups and friends have heard numerous occasional poems, most of which I have assumed outside general interest and therefore, have not included in this collection.

Most intimate family includes my beautiful daughters, Hilary and Ariana, and my beautiful wife Mary. They have seen me up close almost daily through the years that I have written most of the poems included in this collection. Mary has had especially great influence on my writing. She seems to have an uncanny ability to tell me what I need to hear. I often dismiss her feedback only to awaken to it a few hours later. Thence I incorporate many of her suggestions. My daughters both write lyrics and music. I am gratified and encouraged when they attribute their creative interest in part to their experience of their father's writing.

A long line of valuable teachers has blessed me. From grade school, through high school, college, medical school, psychiatric residency and beyond, this chain of great teachers is unbroken. Currently my teachers include shamans named Judy and Armand. Their methods are mysterious. Their intentions are clear. Their impact is immense. My Zen teachers, Nicolee Keiren Jikyo McMahon Roshi, Jake Jiyo Gage Sensei, and Barry Keigen McMahon Sensei of the Three Treasures Zen Community keep me on my toes paying attention to life as it passes. All is koan. All is cause. All is effect.

PART I

SKY: GETTING HIGHER

CONTENTS

MORNING

Perpetual morning
Birds sing at dawn
Sun's rays brighten life
Bodies stretch into day

SUFFER THE SUFFERING

Everything hurts, at least a little bit
Or else it isn't real
Everything hurts more because
we encourage the hurting
by trying to avoid it
trying to make it hurt less
trying not to experience our hurt
Hurting includes our hurting others
We're always hurting others at least a little
Or else it isn't real
We hurt them more by trying to avoid it
by trying to hurt them less,
trying to experience less of their hurt
Such old limiting patterns expend our energy
to maintain themselves
or else they aren't real
They use us, they feed off our energy
They encourage us with fear of future, past shame
To bring past and future into the moment
Polluting the pure presence of the moment
To benefit those old, familiar decision patterns
Every time we repeat the old behaviors
Every time we allow past and future to influence a momentary decision
we strengthen its influence with our energy
Deepening old patterns distance us from ourselves,
prevent our reaching moment's breast
Unable to suck out all the marrow from the moment;
the strength, breadth, width and depth;
missing moments' unique vibration
The color, the tone, subtlest nuance of moment;
can surround us, support us, sooth us
Perhaps we can learn to swim eternally in the moment;
in the energies flowing through us and over us
Flowing from the elegant art of this only moment

HOLY

what is it that is holy
what is holy is what it is

LET US BOW

let us bow to what blesses us
to receive all of this life's blessings
in the touch of third eye to earth
thence to scoop up her holy water
to anoint our heads

MY SONG

Tonight what I want is just to sing
To sing my song tonight out loud
Toning my "ong" and my "Omm"
To sing of my feet, my face and everything in between
Only to sing of it all right now tonight, my life
Song of Bali and Baltimore, "B" Street and Bombay
Song of Clintons, of Carters remembered and forgotten
Tonight I am in love with all of this
Even my wretched dreams I anticipate with love this night
Loving my song now, my body now, my life now

BEYOND INSTINCT

the body I now inhabit
just another very powerful habit
the very life I now lead
just accumulated habits
cellularly structured in genes and deep memory
it all has its usefulness
it is what it is
it is certainly not all that there is
we are too lightly made to be it all
by design, we last about seventy-odd years
not very long, really
the plan for ageing and death
woven into the basic structure of every cell
programmed into our DNA
that is a heavy habit
a hard habit to break
thanks be, it's only here for a moment
eternal moment come and gone before we even know it
unseen behind the wall of past hurts and future fears
eternal truth in this moment
beyond habit
beyond instinct

JUST THE FACTS

Please, Doctor
My eyes
Take the film away
The film of self
The shell of habit
The story of self
The lenses of knowing
Let me see what is
Just as it is
However it is

Thank you Doctor
I can see clearly
I can connect intimately
With satisfactoriness
Not making it mine
Not seeking cause and remedy
Before seeing the facts
Just the facts ma'am

GRADUAL CLEARING

Following long darkness
Grey cloud to skyward
Dense fog straight ahead
Thick marine layer persists
Between me and clear blue

Here comes gradual clearing
Intervals of brightened sky
At first disbelieved midst lingering haze
Easily dismissed in mindful context
Embedded in mankind's eternal dimness
Brightness' fleeting blush aids this cynic

Perfection's phantom shines in darkness
When I take phantom's siren song into my heart
My heart can hold it; my voice can sing it
To make it bigger and better; even good
Clear sky shines on songs sung from heart space
Heart's pure light perfects human song

My heart beats like the wings of the wren
That flies into a window at one end of the Great Hall
Ancient Norse image for the beginning of life
Wren flies purposefully through warmly lighted chamber
Then flies out a window at the other end of the hall

From whence comes this breathing heart's energy
To where does it disappear when it leaves
These questions emerge in my human life's flight
Questions that vanish in clear aura of open heart
Persistent clear light that, like the wren in the Great Hall
Transcends this enclosure I call my life

GRACE PLACE

From somewhere deep inside
Core of being, core of ground
From somewhere like this
Grace Place

Grendel, his mother, and the dragon
Out of unspeakable gales of grief
Threatening monsters claim me
Grace Place

Contained only in this dance
Maintained only by its music
In somewhere like this
Grace Place

Only in this now life of mine
Uniquely me, all by myself
Greatly self, mountain being
Grace Place

Here stars in my heart's love
Hear this voice, God in me
Living in my eternal sun
Grace Place

DESCENT INTO MYSTERY

The lights go down
Who knows what we will find
In the dark, right here in the dark
This mystery now is mine to keep
Where was I?
Where did I come from?
What am I?
What have I become?
How is this life?
How is it here now?
Where am I going?
Where is this 'I' I have become?
Where is this 'me' that I am?
Mystery informs me
Tells my heart to tell me
Here, now, I am signified
Tells my feet to tell me
Here, now, I am home

ABSURDITIES

Dance without dancers
Sound without vibration
Light without a source
Order without a plan
Matter without energy
Belief without faith
Life without love

SUMMIT

While we climb
We are there
Snow capped
Wind swept
Serenely majestic

When we have gained it
We gaze beyond our perch
To ocean's horizons
From whence we've ascended
We are there too

So in solitude
We dream
The wind blows
We remember
Myth warms us

Lining the dream
Our heartbeat echoes
From distant peaks
We stretch above the sun
Extend below ocean's floor

Nurtured by beauty
Complete within
Center blossom's fragment
Unifies itself
Reifies all

PERCHANCE TO DREAM

Sleep is also called for by this life
How to maintain the dream
Dreaming a totally awakened beingness
Only to sleep
Perchance to dream

HAILSTORM

Enlightenment comes at me
Like a gentle spring zephyr
Taunting and teasing my surface
Inspiring me to wish more deeply

A freshening falls upon me
Now bearing an aroma of apple
Sweet smells stimulate other senses
Eyes awaken sight, ears awaken sounds

So awakened, enlightenment is constant
Enlightenment pours in upon me
Like a sudden summer shower
Little hailstones demanding attention

Enlightenment pours on me in warm rays of sun
Energy of sun's constant combustion
Myriad material forms; rose buds and 350Z's
Bear sun's energy in structured molecule

Living earth, breathing cosmos
Dancing all for my pleasure
All of life for my enlightenment
Including the moment of my death

For what of this moment is not life?
For what of this moment is not love?
For what of this moment is not now?
For what of this moment is not hail?

Defeat and triumph depend on each other for existence
Faith and doubt, treasure and tribulation
In and out, light and darkness
Temporal and timeless, sacred and profane

All of it only here now in this moment's stimulation
All of it in sparsely spaced, brilliant green leaves
As they spread out along this tree's long limbs
Glowing in the backlight of morning sun
Elegant form unites with elegant function
Reaching together for sunlight, fuel for all life

NOWHERE

nowhere to go to find it
nowhere to go to hold it
nowhere to go to be with it
just right here

just this now
just this moment
just this person
just this you

ECLIPSE

Composed during the total solar eclipse
July 11, 1991
The nineteenth anniversary of Jennifer's death

Birds sing their night songs as
Ultimately dusk settles over the land.
People with mirrors and white paper
Protect their eyes with exposed film.

I walk on the shore, barefoot in the sand.
Warm waves gently caress my feet.
This experience of this day is like no other.
It can never be told completely.

Try counting the fleas in shifting sand
Or the clouds of queen fist schooled in kelp.
Try to predict the height of each wave.
Will it reach the rock upon which you rest?

Death lies in this sand; small ray decomposing,
Partially skeletonized bird, species indefinite.
As I return, I find my shoes and socks
Where I left them on the sand pile.

What is it like to die?
Imagine it!
A blunt, soft edge like the gentle lap
Of quiet sea on subtle slope of sand;
Brief dimness followed by brighter day.

WISCONSIN

not in cardinal and white
badger colors for which we rooted
but true green of grass
true blue of sky
bluer still of lake
Wisconsin in June
so seductive

THIS TIME

I can hear and I can see
there was a time when I
could climb the highest tree
upon all of that I swear
doing is a big part of me
working harder, digging deeper
only to find all of it free

DEEP LIGHT

candle's gentle light flickers in slight breeze
its small flame easily extinguished
leaving behind its small shadow space
darkening the cave it formerly lighted

our candles connected create a zealous fire
generate an inferno the storm can only fan
community of candles, a blazing conflagration
bright through long night 'til dawn's fingers appear

father and mother, source of all light, the sun
burns furiously, uninterrupted
exemplary source of flame, heat and light
consuming itself, generous, certain, secure

sun laughs its flames far into the cosmos
creating elements from which all becomes
millions more burn as brightly at a distance
listen to them laugh from night sky's sheltering net

SAY YES

It's true, it's true
Everything is new
All this beauty
All this pain
All of it resides in you
Ever new, ever new
Everything is new
There is nothing for us to do
Nothing except say, "Yes"!

How can I stand it?
How can I survive?
Like the amoeba flows
Surround life and eat it
Be eaten by your life
Eat this moment and be eaten
The snake that swallows its tail

Now I think
Now I am lost
Now there are words
Now I am over here
Now it is over there
There is nothing for us to do
Nothing except say, "Yes"!

It's true, it's true
Truth will wipe your tears
Beauty will blow your nose
Love will be there, it's here
It's all right, it's all right
There is nothing for us to do
Nothing except say, "Yes"!

GOLDEN MOMENTS

Always within me
Dark, rich, creamy
Milk-light chocolate
Belgian, crunchy and cold
Covering almonds, encasing cherries,
honeycomb and caramel
Hershey, Ghirardelli, icons all
Only needing to be seen
No need to be touched
Remembrance is enough
Every echo of what was
Creates what is and what will be
Right here, right now, in me

Imagine a stage set for me
Imagine setting that stage
Then imagine going out into the lights
There to dance egolessly
Growing into myself
Creating my whole dance

Perhaps I can see my dance
Perhaps even dance my dance
Golden moments dance around me
Golden moments dance within

Like lonely strands of DNA
Wanting desperately to create themselves
Each helpless without four fingers in threes
Sequencing bits of itself for combining

GOLDEN MOMENTS
continued

When I create stages of myself I believe my plan
My specific pre-conception sufficient and valid
Able to see my life as simply DNA
Unable to see my larger work unfolding
Exercising its intention to play with itself
Creating chains of golden moments

Imagine something that big and that good
Some incredible, self-replicating ribbon of gold
Mobius-like in its one-sided eternity
Surrounding me, within and without

Memory's gold intrigues me with its weight and substance
Inviting me to consider my body's life worth wanting
Worth staying here for, worth being here for
Dancing on my side of Mobius singularity
Looping before me in its endless, twisting road

From fear I cling to my golden road
From ignorance of spaceless space
Barely am I able to hold on
As formless, mindless emptiness embraces me

Entry into emptiness brings freedom with my first step
Nothing remains to be feared
Golden moments, now free for becoming
Golden moments, ever free for being

SPINNING

Sitting on a rock
Feeling gentleness breeze caress
Brown and blue and grey surround me
Familiar patterns, earth, and sky
Seen clearly by ancient ones in this place
Patterns seen by their changing

Ceaseless change shown in shadows lengthening
Coalescing into dusk
Changing sky as our earthly home spins
Candles burn slowly soon to fizzle out in their holders
Life's energy rises and falls within me
Living and dying within and all around

Then it's the pink sky
Wisping over head above fiery horizons
Almost completely surrounding us
Pink becoming red to the west
Browns and blues and greens fade
Becoming pinkness, then redness
Then gray, all grays, then black
Except for countless pinholes of white
Shining down upon us as we spin on

FLYING HIGH

I easily admit to knowing
There's no way for me to know
Something I know I know
I'm always afloat in something

Too constant to comprehend
I'm the hawk flying in infinite air
Salmon swimming in measureless sea
Afloat in immensely spaced depth

Vast robe around and part of me
Bone and sinew extending
Outside hearing, beyond seeing
Beyond imagination

Still some strange knowing, known
Some extra sense informs me
I am sea as well as salmon
I am sky as well as hawk

Through all time I have floated
I'll remain always afloat
I know I'm this infinite ocean
Aware I'm the air where I float

PART II

SEA: SPREADING OUT

CONTENTS

INVITATION

You invite me and I am afraid
I am afraid to go to my holy place
I am afraid to be there in that space
My own dance, mine alone
And it frightens me
How can it be, how can it be
After all I am free, I am free
I am uniquely me
Dance to that freedom
This me-dom
The invitation stands midst the rhythm
Within the restraint
Inviting music
Inviting dance
Inviting this….
My dance
My love

ALL'S IN THE WATER

So you are looking for the most interesting life you can find
Scanning distant horizon for what is closest to you
Chasing a life you already own
The most interesting life ever lived
Water to drink, water to surf on
Water for cleaning ourselves
Water to grow things we need
Water to swim in
Water to float on
Water to appreciate
To dive into
Tasting, smelling, feeling the water
Knowing water, knowing ourselves

SEARCHING

when searching ceases
when I no longer search
when I am just the searching

then I am myself
then I am swept away
then I know who this me is

.

RUNS WITH RIVERS

Having arrived in this world
Beneath a Virgo-shaped sky
Inheriting at once this earthly sign
Ever challenged to fly, burn, and flow

In Bali's open sky, new constellations arise
In her clean, sweet air, passions burn brighter
Abundant water flows in her streams and sluices
Mindfully managed to produce rice for her people

Water barely moves through her ancient terraced hills
Inviting me to free myself from solid earth
Pulling me out from firmly fixed roots
First to imagine, finally flowing, not fixed nor free

Her water subtly seduces me
To abandon my more structured form
Not yet to fly nor burn but to run with rivers
Today I rename myself, "Runs With Rivers"

BIG WATER

Like a rock in rushing water
Ever so gradually eroding to sand
In turn washed down to big water
Neither asked nor asking the reason
Neither knowing where it belongs nor where it goes

You cannot believe the trouble I've seen
No more than I can know yours
But we cannot choose whether we dance
Only the music, the style of our moves

Still we will go wherever our lives take us
While we determine some turns in our paths
Arabesque, en pointe, plie
Leaping high and long
Individual, independent, series and runs

It's the song that finds its way into my soul
The song that becomes my soul
The song that causes my feet to dance
All along the way, from rock to sand, to distant, vast sea

Please don't go away, don't ever go away
Please stay how you are, where you are
Please don't succumb to water's wearing
Don't change a hair, not if you care
Though I know we must
We must wear ourselves away
Dancing our way to ever bigger water

SOAKED

a grey-haired man walks
a grey old dog in gentle rain
neither seems to hurry
maybe they want plenty of time to get wet
they seem to soak up the rain
like sponges, they'll dry soon enough
they pass out of my headlights
again they belong to the night
I am left with impressions, memories
witness to my own experience
steeped in my own unique brain juices
to me of doubtful value
to the universe, pure treasure

ON BEING FREE

Until now, I never understood why he made of me such a celebrity
Telling every successive class of my contribution
It was a discussion of the dilemmas of a democracy
Probably triggered by Tocqueville's *Democracy in America*
I responded to what I heard as elitism and Euro centrism
No matter how you are gifted, I said, you can still be a, "good guy"
I believed it then and I continue to believe it
Given sufficient opportunity, common men, common women
can as easily raise the average as can kings
Those who settled these shores were surely common men
The savior worshipped by Christians was surely a common man
Common in the sense of being "not of nobility"
Uncommon as to vision and commitment to principle

The professor's problem wasn't with being a good guy for he was one
The professor's problem was about what, "being a good guy" meant
My personal definition in no way conflicts with being one's best
Being one's best must include consideration of resources
One's situation needs first to be known
Knowing the other is essential to being your best
Knowing the other is essential to being yourself

When we listen mindfully to our lives, we hear a whisper
A life that whispers compassion can be heard
Such a life spoken in words can be shared
How much the life of affect and affection goes unappreciated
The action of a teardrop shed in compassionate togetherness
can be swallowed up in the droning moment
Either word or tear offered from a need to please the other
Ghostly, without substance, pale, devalued and forgotten
So it is with word or tear propelled by a need to please the self
Just another ghost lurking about pretending to be present
Rendering our words heartless, other than
Robbing our expressions of their life
Undistinguished, indistinguishable
Another lost self, another lost soul
Trying to become average, to become the same as
Trying to please a whole we can never hope to know

ON BEING FREE
continued

Willing to be the same as nothing that exists
Able to accept the present of our presence
That's the way into the garden of our lives
A garden where everything is growing
We can just sit back and watch it grow
Celebrate with cigarettes and ice cream
If you really want 'em they can only help you grow
Dancing in your garden with joy
Another lost soul dancing with another lost spirit
Together at last, all one needs
Dancing in this right-here-now body
Dancing in this right-here-now place
Dancing in this right-here-now time

There is a light off there in the corner
If you try real hard, you can see it too
That is the light wherein I dance
Growing this light until it becomes everyone's
Growing this light until it becomes everything
Growing the light until I become nothing, Amen
You are dancing too, here with me
Alleluia to our soul, Alleluia to the one

SO SOON SPENT

How easily we change one another into ghosts
Some eerie presence, some befogged image
Just a promise, just a little sniff, a lick
We learn to play it safe
Clinging to some imagined certainty
Certainty that can be only imagined
What we live with mostly is flow
Sea or river, lake or pond
Like water life flows
Or it dies and disappears

Nothing we can imagine could be less certain
Than our lives right now
We don't have to imagine fear
We don't have to imagine grief
We instead create ghosts of ourselves
Characters to stand in for us
Understudies, stunt men, acrobats
Those daring young men on the flying trapeze
Alarming presences of power beings, these Gods
Others to play our parts
All the while we know nothing about any of it
We remain ghosts creating other ghosts
Our lives could really become us
This life so recently received
This life we shall so soon see spent

CHRISTMAS REMEMBERING

Christmastide traditions bring memories
Striking memories, vivid and profound
Memories of people inform me who I am
Memories of people no longer of the flesh

Just about the time I get what I want
I forget what I wanted, I forget why I wanted it
What I always thought I wanted was
To tend the family fire, feed the family's fire

Tradition drinks me in to its steady warmth
As I become a part of it, the veil thins
What was, now enfolded in me, lives yet again
Enfolded inheritance, this beast ignores change

Names like Mabel, Gladys, Gordon, Ethel, and Alice
John and Rob, Paul and Clifford Isadore
Margaret, dear Margaret, poor Margaret
Names like Howard and Lloyd, Lon and Mary Lou

CHRISTMAS REMEMBERING
continued

Voices of parents, cousins, uncles, and aunts
Dare I recall dear departed daughter, Jenny
I remain yet a sensitive boy who hears their voices this moment
Their voices so familiar saying words that might be said

Look at what you have done, accomplished and endured
Imagine what you can do, all you will do
This gift brought to me this Christmas
Courtesy of the great gift we name life

The greatest gift is love
Loving what is right up close
Hugging close to us what we love
Remember, too, how all changes in a moment

Hope, faith, and love, of these three
Love alone can abide in memory's cocoon
Here survives love's voice, a bridge to hope and faith
My Christmas ever lasting with its legacy of love

ENCHANTED FOREST
Jennifer's Return

In this high Himalayan forest everything is changed
Giant rhododendron tower overhead into thinning air
Muted by omnipresent, thickly matted moss
Moss softened rocks beckon saying, "Sit, pilgrim, sit!"

Illusion and reality fuse, inseparable in soft light
Hushed voices, fellow trekkers barely noticed in the distance
When suddenly, the veil lifts, her intimate presence obtrudes
Presence unseen, unheard, yet certain and familiar

Walking with me in this private, silent, sweet softness
Bouncing along off the trunks of magnolia trees
Off softened rocks and stumps and fallen logs
Off my trekking colleagues, unknowing of my experience

For hours, her sweetly present majesty delights me
A lifetime of tears stream hotly down my cheeks
While the forest reflects her, the forest it remains
Enchanted illusion, muted material, momentary, inseparable

Ever after I shall recall this special knowing
The forest, her presence is equally real
Blended in memory, bonded eternally
This forest, this trek, this life goes on and on

WARMING

to goldfish or mouse
a house is just a house
to us it's a different bit

a glass house is nice
if there is not too much ice
and no one is throwing stones at it

warm home made of wood
make it warmer still, we could
by filling its space with the love of it

UPWELLING
Early 1980's

Midst frigid sea, warm currents rise
thawing a more frigid clime
Gulf stream forced deep, wells up immense
from distant place and time

Like tundra vast, forever locked ice
cannot believe in a thaw
But mankind can experience depth
from whence spring wonder and awe

Gratefulness fills and lifts out self
Thanks, this convection brings
Moist eyes signal its upwelling
Gratitude thaws: it sings

What's this warm breeze? Where's its warm source?
Will it go away soon?
A heart so warmed will soar and float
much like a hot air balloon

Soaring provides a wide vista
beyond where heart and hopes sank
Belief in a god is believing
in something or someone to thank

DEEP LIMERICK

Delve into the dark, delve deep
Descend to your depths in your sleep
See the way all things are, both near and far
As along life's winding road you slowly creep

The slime that attracts you, no need to panic
Slide down freely into primordial muck organic
Just a few steps from beach where you stand
You are swept into chaos so magnificent, so grand

Far beyond the muck and the mire
Far beyond the ten thousandth pyre
You may find once again your Arthurian chin
As you swim out to meet yet dearer kin

LITTLE BIRD

Like breath, little bird sings love
Sings God's song in his own throat's song

Sometimes you don't have to say anything
Sometimes you don't have to do anything
Sometimes you don't have to be anyone
Sometimes you don't have to be anywhere
But forever and always, you have to love

Little bird sings, "Life is a lovely thing"
Life is full of all things, let 'em be, let 'em all be
Then your life can be as full as a robin's song

Like breath, little bird sings love
Sings God's song in his own throat's song

There are many lifetimes
We live them all right now
Reincarnation in this moment
Becoming all space, being all beings

Like breath, little bird sings love
Sings God's song in his own throat's song
Little bird says, "Life is a lovely thing"
Life is full of all things imagined
Let 'em be, let 'em all be
Then life will be full, like robin's song

There are many lifetimes
We sing them all right now

MYSELF

Seeing what is, as it is
Life's most interesting challenge
Blinded by peculiarly unique DNA
Bonded to life-long habits assumed
Engraved in self-enforcing networks
Favoring continued seeing
Things as I have seen them before

Freeing myself from this prison
Self-deluded addiction to illusion
Self-inscribed view pretended
Observation distorted, intended
Intention, pretension blotted out
We are windows pretending to be doors
Doors we can close and lock

To keep us safe within supposed secure space
Unable to see through dark-stained, paneled oak
Seeming to secure our boundaries
Protecting precious particularities
Peculiarly personal preconceptions
Preventing perfection's peering
Through clear window of egoless self

AFTER A READING

I sit and recall the feelings, the wonder recalled
The poets recall the wonder, remind the wonderer
We are here now, together in our separateness
We are here now, love, lovers in love, loving

Find your own way, that's what the poets say
I want to cry out to them, thank you
For bringing me new ears and new tongues
For reminding me of deep, knowing wonder
Deep grief deeper love
Deep joy, deeper love
Deep life, deeper love

I want to turn and bow to you poets
Before I turn again to bow to the wall
Then assume my place on my cushion
Now become you, I recall my own love
Now become you, I recall my own wonder
I am both alive and dead, I am here and I am not

WAITING ROOM BLUES

These waiting room blues
Got me thinkin' bout some brews
Lookin'at my shoes
Waitin' for some news

Flight's not in yet
Thought it was all set
But waitin's all I get
Expectations still unmet

Waitin' for my dinner
Instead of eager winner
I'm feelin' like a sinner
Maybe I'll get thinner

Whether waitin' for the call
or linin' up at the mall
For an empty parking stall
Still tryin' to stand tall

Got me up against the wall
Feelin' like some scum ball
Still, I'll be givin' it my all
If I'm still waitin' in the fall

Gadot doesn't come
Of him there's not a crumb
Guess I'll have another rum
Still no sign of the bum

WAITING ROOM BLUES
continued

A finger and a thumb
Means I'm not all that dumb
With a fee-fi-fo-fum
Maybe I can get me some

Of what I'm waitin' for
On some far and distant shore
Then I'd only want some more
Waiting's such a bore

Instead of gettin' sore
I'll be headin' for the door
that leads inward to my core
So that's what waitin's for!

WHAT NEXT

Author, author
Everyone please rise
Author of future
By whom is it written?

All bylines forgotten
Only words survive
Only words that come to me
Never mine except in saying

What a word signifies
Neither is this thing mine
Only mine in meeting
Myself going into the world
Myself coming out again

My own life
Neither is it mine
Only as it comes to me
Only as I meet it

Hand over hand
Heaving the anchor
Link by heavy link
Drifting into my long voyage

Depths unknown
Plumbed in the command
Away anchor!
Into a sea that knows itself

Sailing out with the wind
Beating out against it
Stars lead me on
Wind, Sail, Sea, and I are one

What's next is right here now and passing
Before I can claim it, what's next is past
Chain of nexts now coming, now going
Nexts in ceaseless waves float me on

ROOTS

What will the neighbors think?
If he can't sell himself how can he sell his line?
He constantly works on his display
Striving to look shiny and polished
Never mind the putrid, black soul spots
The heart of stone
Forget about it
Hawk the light
Sell the sweetness

Get this boy off the farm
Away from the barn
With its stink of life's excretions
But still he wears his stinking barn shoes
Poor boy
The only pair he has
Dead give away for this hick from the sticks
Roughing his road to success

Suddenly he sees his stinking shoes as roots
Suddenly he knows the needed nourishment they bring
Suddenly his soul becomes whole
Suddenly his heart softens
Suddenly this truth penetrates his cover-up

Now he knows
He is as shiny as he needs to be
The spit and polish can stop
The selling can cease
Newfound roots render these efforts needless
Let the neighbors think what they will

TRAINING WHEELS

the day we took them off, we were excited
she scared, me anxious
would she be able to balance without them
were her regulatory mechanisms sufficient
her brain mature enough to replace ancillary balancers
had she enough time, enough experience
matured by outrigger wheels

that's what they're for, I said
just to get you started
after that they get in the way
they slow you down; they can be dangerous

unconvinced, she wobbled down the sidewalk
twice she ran into neighbor's yards
once almost into a rail fence, but she didn't fall
we were very proud

when I was a boy, there were no training wheels, said I
my mother held on to the back of the seat
and gave me a push when she thought I was ready
I rode. I wobbled. Still do a bit

parents are like these little wheels
we balance, we stabilize, then let go and watch
when they're ready to ride alone
when we're ready to let them

we get scared too, right along with them
when we know they're out of our control
no training wheels except the ones they've developed within
just the ones that don't show
except when we let go

BUTTERFLY

as I walk along this desert path
here so widely cleared of plants and rocks
finely ground sand drenched in brilliant sun
screen where I encounter erratic darting on desert dust before me
unmistakable, butterfly's shadow appears

I casually glance upward to find such shadow's cause
I can see no butterfly flitting above me
resigned to impossible severance of cause from effect
resigned to spending my time walking in life's shadows
still incessant shadow's motion invites continued attention
again and again, fleeting peeks fail to disclose her presence

at last I stop my walking, remove my billed cap
at last I seriously seek to see unseen shadow-caster
at last I see what must have been above me all along
at last I witness butterfly's colorfully patterned substance
freely swimming through vast blue of desert's summer sky

to earnestly seek the root of clues I clearly witness
to quit moving on, to remove thought's cap, to notice
to take love seriously enough to see it here
as its shadow flits before me in the dust of my life
dancing on this ground of being I walk upon
shadowy substance of all loves, I see here again
on late summer's stroll with this remarkable young woman
this beautifully elegant, intelligently radiant young woman
whom I have loved unconditionally
ever since before she was born

TURNING WORD

a word that turns
a thought, a wish
an idea that's caught
in your net like a fist

your idea, your net
let it go if you wish
let it turn toward freedom
give freedom to fish

free turning toward
or turning away
turning's the thing
fish turns show us the way

turn, turn and turn
tight radius they've found
'bout a tenth of their length
it takes them to turn 'round

no wonder the fish symbol
adorns bumper ahead
abounds in our culture
look where turning has led

turning reminds us
the turn is the thing
whether toward or away
in their turning, bells ring

PERHAPS JOY

we call it life
this breathing
this breath of being
some call it, "Breath of God"
or, "Sea of God's Love"
where we are safely borne afloat
where eternally we swim

perhaps it is joy
primal joy of life
joy wherever we are
joy in shame and rage
joy in sadness, in loss
joy of life yet in death

just being in joy
just breathing joy in and out
exhaling, inhaling existence
learning to enjoy all of it
deciding to enjoy everything
breathing our own joy
all the time

PART III

EARTH: THE PURPOSE OF ORCHIDS

CONTENTS

NIGHT RIDER

Who makes my rider ride?
Who lets my rider ride?
Why can't I be seen like I want to be seen?
Inner begets outer
I am the rider who terrifies me
I am the rider I defend against
I recoil at such simplicity
My defenses prevent what I desire
My armor prevents my being seen
Fear of being ridden in darkness by the rider I create
Prevents spontaneous joy from arising out of my life

PUS WORDS

don't you love when the words come oozing out
much like pus from a draining wound
a newly lanced boil or carbuncle
spirit wounded, self-inflicted
spirit willingly infected with life

OF ANIMALS AND ORCHIDS

On the purpose of orchids and the influence of dogs
To be seen

Beauty and playfulness
Both requiring a retard in the cadence of my purposeful gait

Alas, poor eyes, trained in only one direction
Wealthy ears immersed in warm constant
Three-sixty surround of glorious sound

Attention, Attention
Pay attention to dog
See orchid illumined
Ineffably fragile beauty
Her white blooms bathed in diffuse, pale, twilight rays
A sight, when noticed, well worthy of a complete stop, total focus

Hear the rapid repetition of slap, slap, slap
Dogs rope toy clenched tightly in her iron jaws
Shaken viciously with growls
Convincing herself, over and over
It shall not escape, it shall not escape

Nor shall I should she choose to grasp me thus
Pay attention to all possibilities
Three-sixty surround of the possible

ANGEL DUST

Ducks splash wildly in twilight's channel
Seeming to relish their unplanned play
Their names must be something like innocence
Here am I, innocence, here with you now

I used to answer only to "Jim"
Now I feel called by all names
It is difficult not to believe in angels
When you discover you are one

If I am an angel then so must you be
When we come to know how we are made
        and of what
As dust whirls up from an open field
Spirit breath gathers, spins our dust into clay

Like snowflakes and fingerprints, infinite clays
As birds in flight cause us to look up
Clay compels us to cast our gaze downward
Down to the details, the small things like ourselves

Our soft clay can be worked by hands, unseen
As life's wheel lovingly turns us
Potential untold, shape and color unknown
When we create ourselves, we are too soon formed

Forgetting who we are and of what we are made
Forgetting delusions built in by design
We choose our glaze when we think our form hardened
We forget our protean shapes, our potential names

When I was growing up I also grew down
So please call me Clay or else call me Dusty
I'll answer, sweet Ma Ma. I'll answer, sweet bird song
I'll answer, sweet angel, sweet clay, or sweet dust

DRAGON LADDER

Fearsome heat, odiferous to the extreme
Stiletto-sharp teeth rip flesh from bone
Flesh that's cooked simultaneously
In dragon breath's fire
Thence to be ingested with dragon-like delight

What is there here to make me not afraid?
How could I meet such a fearsome beast?
Almost certain doom, gruesome end
Such certainty, the core of the unbeliever
Knowing what follows an unknown death
Sudden darkness, nothing more
All pleasure and all pain is finished
Ended with the last breath of life
Live for the long-range interests of those who follow
For me it will all be over, with the last beat of my heart

And if there is more, then it is more that there is
Not knowing anything about right or wrong
Ignorant of heaven or hell, light or dark
All concepts, merely ideas captured by our culture
Woven into a seamless network to entrap us
Into believing in someone else's idea of truth
Truth too, only a concept that dwells in my mind
Then none of us can know truth beyond the moment
Known only in the millisecond of neuron's firing
All else is supposition, imagination, book knowing
Dictionary, Thesaurus, Bible, Qur'an, Torah or Sutra

DRAGON LADDER
continued

Important knowing is life learning only I can know
Only waves of insight crawling up the sand that is I
Followed by denial's receding surge
With incoming tide of practicing life
Comes higher wave; higher returning wave
Working my way up the ladder that is me
Hearing higher sounds, feeling higher senses
Learning about what is higher in me
Valued charkas, all quite wonderful in their proper place
My proper place is continual movement from one to seven
Caudal to cephalic; energy moving higher and higher

This is what Freud discovered
He told us and he told us
Life is all fucking until you die
Fucking pleasure
Wiggling on up the ladder of pleasure
Fucking life with my mind, then my spirit
Then fucking life with my soul

Jesus told us the same thing
"Turn the other cheek!", isn't about just being good to others
"Blessed are the peacemakers!", isn't just for others
"Blessed are they that mourn!", means you
Well, who are you?
Just an old La Jolla guy who isn't sure he wants to be here
Just an old griever who knows he is here
Only one who receives the gift of his life

CHUNKY LOVE

Tiny bubbles in the champagne of being
Tiny chunks in the liquor of life
We easily see the bubbles
We readily see the chunks
How come we miss the surrounding spirits?
When it's this missing that brings all our funks

To come to know this sublime soup
Wherein all bubbles and chunks reside
To wonder within our love's chunk
Then to leave this place, leave behind the chase
To know omnipresent energy that cannot be sunk

More easily said than done, this leaving
Oh me, what will become of me, oh me

EXCUSED

I may be excused, if I may be excused
But by whom do I consider being excused?
From whom do I wish such complete control?
In this Now time, this no time, no place place
I am already excused
There is nothing but excuses
There is nothing to excuse
Except for the accusations, the false accountings
Tell me it's all funny, tell me it's all a game
I need to know what's going on
I can only know what I want
When I really do my very best
To know what's going on here
For what I cannot yet know
I may be excused

TEST DRIVE

play that which is not so well known to you
now it is time to learn different rhythms, new times
now no one can say why
now it is time to explore where no man has gone before
encounter the world
but that is far too small
encounter space
still not enough for this moment
for that would be outer space
when now we need to claim inner
take life out for a drive
you already own it
see what she'll do

HORSES

Careening carts across narrow streets
Breaking doorways in stores
Threatening commerce
Drawn by crazy horses
Who both know and do not know
Who build and destroy simultaneously

Horses by the team, together in their collar
Learning to pull in a similar direction
Their yoke, their vector equalizer
Makes it hard for them to deviate
Beyond the onset of this pain
Too hard to hurt as much as this

Refusing to be ravished by this life
Results in being ravished by another
Horses here, horses now, horses of this life
Horses learning to be like themselves
Hauling their lives, sounding their joy
In their whinnies, their barks, and their words

Horses of power pull me where I will go
To peaks, to valleys, to places of my power
Rebelling, revolting, resisting it all grandly
Habitual behavior, largely unseen and unknown
Sheep and wolves, 'mongst herds of wild horses

CURSE

All this death stuff can eat you up
Karl Appel played with color and cats
Death can sting you; stop you in your tracks
Mine is a life I can play with

How bad am I to ask for play
To play with my food, my sex, and my life
Walk the beach instead of walking the line
Is play what it is; of course, it is play
Is my life what it is; of course, it's my life
My life; it's own answers to its own questions

It's a big life, here in this little house of mine
It's a big life in a little person; in a little time
Such a little time spreads out over great expanse
Such a greatness of being
so surprised to see it all again
so easy to forget
so important to recall
storied something
stymied, stifled,
shuffled into an enormous deck
some outrageous curse causes

The curse, of what is it wrought?
The curse, wherein its cure
The curse, wherein its ending
The curse, wherein I play

FOR MOTHERLESS ONES

Choices to be made before they disappear
Choices cascade in continuing cadence
Crashing, careening, crumbling upon the floor
Strewn chaotically clear over to the door

Is this a good marriage; am I in the right work?
Is this my home, this place where I live?
Is my life as good as it should be?
Am I as good as I should be?

Choices litter our minds like unmade beds
Well, I really should make that bed
Choices like these block entry into fields more vast
Multiply in brains' dark canyons

For brief moments, I can choose
Brief moments of knowing my choosing
To choose not choosing; complete experience
To choose this moment's momentous mystery

As close as I can come to bird's flight
Hopped out of nest; coming to trust wings
Motherless child, free and far from home
Hard times require heart's discipline
Kingdom Come; Thou shalt not kill
Thought or word or deed; My own or that of another

ALMOST PARADISE

Tonight the lake was circumscribed by
Sunset on our right, rainbow on our left
and lightning show in the center ring
This circus is one of beauty, majesty
Huge beauty of mountain and sky
Moving waters of rivers, lakes, and streams
Song birds familiar, species unknown
Birds of prey seldom seen by many
Bears black and bears grizzly
Pristine wilderness where river rafters
Can't move a snag or strainer in the wild river
Without making an environmental impact study
But something in this perfection of nature
Gnaws deeply into my gut
Perhaps it's the undeniable impact of man's presence
As he creates his world of convenience
Changing wilderness into strip malls
Serene lakes becoming cacophonies of frothing caldrons
Civilization multiplies along with its varied forms of dirt
While the wilderness shrinks
Both of these are my nature
Wilderness and civilization are both myself

SOLITARY

Confinement, always the safest
Slave's quarters still feel good
Confinement, someone's idea of good for real
Confinement, close, convenient, familiar
Never cool to try to look cool

Feeling the freedom
No longer craving confinement
I never wanted to hurt you like this
Genuine, cool, sweet sea breeze caresses
I never wanted to hurt me like that
Sun shines warm on ripening roses

Freedom is in the trees
Fearless in their branching
Including all of these
Neurons, brain's slow silicon chips
Nothing spectacular in themselves
But oh, the connections they make

The truth is in your trees
Do whatever you wish
Eternal heaven remains your dish
Nothing you can do about it
Except to create all the beauty you can
Heaven on earth
In this life; in this life

MYTH OF KINGS

Bucket of flowers in foreground
Bougainvillea as backdrop
Remarkable rightness, uncanny contentment
Here, now, round and whole
Where I will go, fantasy and plans
All of it in this place, right now
Sensate image replaces idea
Old narratives drown in this instant
Princely peace becomes me, blessed
Now become king, here I am blessing
Bougainvillea climbs to the rooftop unnoticed
Each blossom being only its own beauty
Rooting, seeking light, expressing itself
Each blossom glorious, each its own king

For long enough now we have dreamed
Hoping for good kings on this earth
Hoping for good kings in the heavens
Kings who will slay our dragons
Kings who will maximize our talents
Kings who will lead us to glory
Long enough to believe in Arthur
Long enough to believe in Kennedys
Long enough to believe in old gods
We can live with dragons
We can claim our kingship
We can share each life's glory
Now is our time to own life
Now is our time to be here
Now is our time to live life
Now is our time to wake up

NUTSHELL

we must all fall
all of us must fall
before we fall flat
best to fall on our knees
yielding to what is
flattened by truth
humbled before death
after all, we are alive

TO PLAY WITH FIRE

what if this is all there is?
this moment's fire
just this
if this moment's fire is all there is
let me know it well
let me learn to play with it
play, that unique opportunity
to manage and be managed
ashes becoming flame
synchronously
balanced
fire and ice
such extremes
will split solid rock
effortlessly
passion's volcano erupts
cooled by larger senses
cognition
unfairly, dangerously hypertrophied
time to give in a little
to the fire
play me some blues, brother
make it a jazz version
bring in some cognition
for the Devil dwells
within me
along with the love
still in love
with all whom I love
all I have loved
body and soul
life teaches its own lessons
this life that burns within
cell by cell, by cell, by cell

CIRCUS RINGS

time was when I was loved the way I want to be loved
scrawling, bawling, wetting, soiling, helpless lump, loved
even the most intense of present loves
is pastel watercolors
compared to the luminous oils of infancy
multiple dimensions of love seem flattened
when we expect what we cannot have
others can only disappoint

there is another chance for riotous color
where love flows round, within and without
there is an art gallery for this life
with every artist's paintings on display
every sculpture's carvings, all creatures' creations
together, accessible, all in one place

pass it on and give it away
empty yourself and be filled
little cog in the universal clock
your energy, part of that spinning wheel
turn with time
join the circus

BALLS

It takes balls to be a man
It takes balls to make babies
Balls to put up your dukes when threatened
Balls to defend family, home, friends, and community

Most of all it takes balls to live with a woman of power
To recognize such power does not mean she is your mother
Her motherhood, her mothering is not the primary source of her power
She is empowered most when she is a woman and you are a man

It is balls that lead us on the hunt
Balls that bag our quarry and bring it home
Balls that maintain the hunt for greater depth
Hunting for greater connection with your woman

Through our connection with woman
Comes greater connection to all things
The hunt for connection never ends
Balls enlist heart and mind in this hunt

INDIA'S GATE

By the India Gate, a voice says, "Hello Sir!"
Just a dignified, strong voiced hello, assertive
See me, he says. You can't avoid me. I'm here!
See what you've come for, indigestibly raw!
Hot sun, unable to move into the shade
Only able to sit and say, "Hello Sir!"
Only able to gesture with his head
Toward the begging bowl before him
He demands to be taken at one glance
Curly dark hair, coffee-brown skin
Athletic torso sits nearly naked
Short stumps of extremities futilely wiggle
I see but do not acknowledge him
I walk on ignoring his near empty bowl
I avert my eyes, yet his image burns my brain
Heart races, stomach; like I've been kicked
Head full, eyes moist, I look back over my shoulder
There he is looking back at me. "Hello!"
I turn into the crowd as it echoes, "Hello Sir!"
I photograph the gate as we circle around it
"Hello Sir!", of course signals our return
Now ensnared, I drop rupees into his bowl
How many of my rupees will he receive?
Is he too hot in the sun? Isn't he thirsty?
Who put him here? Who feeds, who protects?
If he fell over could he sit upright again?
Who will collect the contents of his bowl?
At the end of the day who will take him away?
Senses assaulted, system assailed
This Pilgrim business confuses, confounds
Futile to say, "Not my place, not my way."
Here is the "not me" I have come for
Like the tiny mirrors in that Mogul's bedroom ceiling
India reflects our helpless forms
Our images commingle in Her vast hologram
Thinking I've circled, I've passed through her Gate

Now my way is his way, India's way
India once entered becomes India never forgotten
Although I don't look him in the eye, we're connected
We survive, helpless together, in our village, this earth!

IMPRIMATUR

The doorway of innocence
Appears to open inward
Admitting careless entry
Just a little push on the place where it says,
"PUSH"
Even the most massive door will swing freely open
Innocence well chosen admits all possibilities

The innocent clutches the egg he once was
Choosing to remain ignorant,
in the face of fearsome things
Fearing things unfamiliar
Thoughts, foreign
Feelings, formless
Fear slams shut the doorway of his innocence

Pinned by his fear
Safe at last
Bolted and locked behind his own door
Pinned to the collector's board
Nevermore to soar on his uniquely patterned wings
No more drifting in the updrafts of spirit's freshening breeze

The innocent fears some paradise, lost
A paradise he can only begin to imagine
His defenses, always on the alert
Refuse unscreened input
Prevent entry of experiences most feared
Most required by him
To nourish his infantile imaginings
Courageous ones forgo entirely the latchkey
that fits the inner lock on the doorway of
innocence

IMPRIMATUR
continued

The wise one sees perfection in all things collected
All things admitted freely through the open door
Just as they are, raw and unprocessed
The wise one breathes in horror and defeat
Breathes out horror and defeat
Signified uniquely with his personal imprimatur

The wise one breathes in awesome beauty
All space and all time
Breathes out his singular significance
Knowing the limits of his knowing
The wise one breathes in these limits as well

Breathes in the fear
Breathes in innocence
Breathes in ignorance
Each breath, bearing his unique fingerprint
Each breath, defined by the limits of himself
Each breathe, for the innocents

THE REAL DEAL

Sometimes it's simple
Simple as getting a rag away from a dog who wants it
I am the dog wanting the rag and the person trying to get it away
Devising magnificent deviances, strategies to succeed at retrieving the rag
While dog hangs on to it as hard as he can and pulls with all his might
And that is the real deal

I can build intricate matrices to contain my desires
Complex lattices like atomic structure or an infinite orchestra of vibrating
strings
Theories I borrow or build to explain how things are before I know how
things are
Myths to put it all together into a story I can comprehend and remember
So I don't have to see that the matrix is the rag that the dog and I both want
And that is the real deal

I want what I want when I want it
I think knowing what I want helps me get it
Still I can't get the rag from the dog because he wants it too
What I know without knowing prevents me from knowing
Almost all my knowledge prevents me form knowing
Almost all my knowledge supports the way I want it all to be
All but the rag and the dog and me as we all are

I collect the caps I seldom wear
The ones I wear a lot, I loose
Bound by the hats I keep, bound by the rag to the dog
I am freed by learning to see how I am, what I crave
Facts about myself that I can observe
And this is the real deal

HOLD

it took nothing less
than life lived like this
to bring me to this place
it will take nothing more
than unremitting courage
in the face of daunting odds
certain defeat

Life will hold me
breathe itself into my body
warm me with it's Holy Fire
until it doesn't
life is breathing itself into my body
warming me with its Holy Fire

I hold with this life
I hold with all that it brings
I hold with life's warmth and breath
I shall hold with life
until I no longer breathe
until I am no longer warmed by its fire

Death is born with life
the inevitable result of life
in such a duel, we can choose sides
life brings us many wonderful things
life always brings death; could it be?
could death be another wonderful gift of life?

Round it out, head it up and let it lead you
abandon all the borders of soul
out of control, out of sight
play all the strings, all the notes
could growing the soul be what we are here for?
now it is time to read Rilke

SPIDER, SPIDER

Tonight I caught myself talking to a spider
She was busy out there spinning her web
Just beginning, only a couple of strands
I addressed her with deepest respect

I told her how beautiful she was
And beautiful she was, beautiful she is
Out there in the dark, spinning her web
I see her in my motion detector light

I can see the dark stripes on her legs
Her full belly she carries, delighted it seems
Planning to work through the night, providing the place
Strangest of all, she answered all my queries

I feared her web was in danger for I pass this way often
Not always aware until I'm shocked and ensnared
Then I can only apologize for my inattention
I vow to her, later tonight, I shall return

I will see which way her web is heading
I can tear it down
Then she'll have a chance for a safer place for her babies
If she tells me to buzz off, I'll respect that too

ROUTE SIXTY-SIX

A shaman's path leads to heart
After practicing extreme empathy
After discovering shamanic nature
Feeling the pain of others mixed with mine
Learning when it is theirs, when my own

This self-hewn path of sharp angles
Curving treacherously, narrow and steep
Slippery footing leads to precipitous drop
Falls become more frequent
Whose pain belongs to whom?
In the face of primal fear's monsters

After multitudes of slips and falls
Encountering others fallen along the way
Some hanging over the edge by their fingers
Rescue attempted will likely lose us both
Yet empathy prevents walking by
So I have sat at a respectful distance
Felt them, recalled them in quiet conversation
Until fingers, weakening from fatigue
Gradually open, losing their grip on the earth
Carefully I slide to the edge to watch
As the shape becomes too small to see
I fall with them, then arise and walk on with them in my heart

I receive their agony in this heart space
Mix it with this heart's happiness
Along the whole path, illumining its dangers
Presenting a way for soul's passage
Heart energy, twenty-four hour relief
As wounds partly healed are again pulled apart

Heart of the healer wherein concepts dance
On sheltering sea, 'neath sheltering sky
Afraid of my song, singing it yet

Dancing with heart's endless energy
Heart's light brightens the dark trip to the sun
Bending South toward West on old Route Sixty-Six

CREMATION

Here I am in an unfamiliar world
Soaking it all in
Sponging it all up
Cymbal and drum
Played by uniformed marchers
Spaced sound, packets of energy
With intricate rhythms and beating chords
Gamelan's discordant quanta infuse the rest

Within our taxi's womb, we join with the rest
We roll down the windows
Invited to enter marchers' magical space
As they slowly move from grave to pyre to river
In the company of loved-ones' bones and ashes
Born on the shoulders of marching men
Transiently entombed in brilliantly colored pyramids
Deities various, imaged and masked
Horned, trunked, fanged, and winged
Some trailing finely painted flame
Soon to rest in fire's final flame
Liberation's hot flame
Soon released to rushing waters
Thence swept beyond earthly substance
Merging with water, becoming the sea

Soon enough we will sleep soundly
On the banks of the roaring river
Constant reminder of our transience
Rushing water carries ashes of countless souls
Once born to human form as are we
Now again unformed and free

Only one breath away we sleep
From ashes suspended in the river
Ashes born to us, then quickly away
As her flowing ceaselessly sings her presence
She reveals her purpose to all who can hear
The sound of water we shall also soon run with

OUT OF HIDING

we are windows pretending to be walls
planets pretending to be pinpoints
so clever at pretense
we cannot find ourselves
once we come out of hiding
oceans cannot contain us
night skies kneel at our feet

BIOGRAPHY OF
JAMES LLOYD RICE

Dr. Rice has been reading poetry for fifty years and writing it for over thirty. He regularly attends readings and reads his work to groups. He has written hundreds of poems. His skills have slowly and steadily improved without formal training beyond college English classes.

He has practiced psychiatry for nearly forty years with training in psychoanalytic theory and has vast experience with a wide variety of patients. His work days consist mostly in listening to his patients tell their stories and trying to understand their situations and life patterns. He does his best work by relating their stories to his own. This practice presents copious material for poetic translation.

Personal life experiences form the other major leg of his writing. In his early adult life, he suffered two crippling losses. His first wife was struck down by immediately disabling multiple sclerosis in their second year of marriage. Ten years later their healthy, lively, bright and beautiful eight year old daughter and only child died of Reyes syndrome following a mild case of chicken pox. Much of his subsequent life has been dominated by his attempts to integrate these tragedies into a satisfying and constructive life. His searching the outer world for support has gradually shifted to searching his inner world. It is here he has been most successful. It is the inner search that is chiefly reflected in his writing.

Born and reared in central Wisconsin, Dr. Rice now lives with his wife of twenty-five years and their young adult daughters in coastal California, forty miles north of the Mexican border. This environment provides abundant beauty with its ocean, deserts, and mountains. It contains a huge and multifaceted population. From this plethora of people he has had the good fortune to gather a large group of true friends.

He has sailed the Pacific and skied the mountains of California, Utah, Montana, and Colorado. His hiking was highlighted by his ascent of Mount

Whitney a month before his sixtieth birthday. He intends to repeat this feat in about two years, on his seventieth. He has traveled extensively in Asia, including Nepal, Thailand, India, China, Japan, and Bali. On his first trip to Nepal he became attracted to eastern thought and spirituality. Zen practice and shamanic teachings have come to enrich his life and his writing and compliment his psychiatric practice as well.

Dr. Rice believes it would be ideal if everyone valued their own life as if it were the most interesting life ever lived. Of all the lives he has known of, in his practice and among friends and family, he has found none more interesting than his own.

978-0-595-35873-1
0-595-35873-X

Printed in the United States
40379LVS00006B/154-201

9 780595 358731